CW00557673

SELECTED POEMS

SELECTED POEMS

Robert Crawford

CAPE POETRY

Published by Jonathan Cape 2005

2 4 6 8 10 9 7 5 3 1

First published in Great Britain in 2005 by
Jonathan Cape
Random House, 20 Vauxhall Bridge Road, London SW1V 2SA

Random House Australia (Pty) Limited
20 Alfred Street, Milsons Point, Sydney,
New South Wales 2061, Australia

Random House New Zealand Limited
18 Poland Road, Glenfield,
Auckland 10, New Zealand

Random House South Africa (Pty) Limited
Endulini, 5A Jubilee Road, Parktown 2193, South Africa

The Random House Group Limited Reg. No. 954009
www.randomhouse.co.uk

'Ah Waant' and 'Day Cowps' are reprinted from *Sharawaggi* (Polygon, 1990) by
Robert Crawford and W.N. Herbert, with the permission of the original publisher

A CIP catalogue record for this book is available from the British Library

ISBN 0-224-07694-9

Papers used by Random House are natural,
recyclable products made from wood grown in sustainable forests;
the manufacturing processes conform to the environmental
regulations of the country of origin

Printed and bound in Great Britain by
Biddles Ltd, King's Lynn, Norfolk

for Alice, Lewis, Blyth

with love

CONTENTS

from *A Scottish Assembly* (1990)

from *Sharawaggi* (1990)

from *Talkies* (1992)

from *Masculinity* (1996)

from *Spirit Machines* (1999)

from *The Tip of My Tongue* (2003)

OPERA

Throw all your stagey chandeliers in wheelbarrows and
    move them north
To celebrate my mother's sewing-machine
And her beneath an eighty-watt bulb, pedalling
Iambs on an antique metal footplate
Powering the needle through its regular lines,
Doing her work. To me as a young boy
That was her typewriter. I'd watch
Her hands and feet in unison, or read
Between her calves the wrought-iron letters:
SINGER. Mass-produced polished wood and metal,
It was a powerful instrument. I stared
Hard at its brilliant needle's eye that purred
And shone at night; and then each morning after
I went to work at school, wearing her songs.

THE SALTCOATS STRUCTURALISTS

for Douglas Cairns

They found the world's new structure was a binary
Gleaming opposition of two rails

That never crossed but ran on parallel
Straight out of Cairo. From small boys

On Platform One who listened to the great
Schola cantorum of connecting rods

Dreamed-up by Scots-tongued engineers, they went on
To tame the desert, importing locomotives

From a distant Firth. New wives came out, and one,
Shipwrecked off Ailsa Craig, returned to Glasgow,

Caught the next boat; her servants had her wardrobe
Replaced in just four hours from the city shops.

Scotsmen among colonial expats
They learned RP, embarrassing their families

In Ayrshire villages where they talked non-stop
About biggah boilahs, crankshawfts. Nicknamed 'The Pharaohs',

They never understood the deconstruction
Visited on Empire when their reign in Egypt

Ran out of steam. They first-classed back to Saltcoats,
Post-Nasser; on slow commuter diesels

They passed the bare brick shells of loco-sheds
Like great robbed tombs. They eyed the proud slave faces

Of laid-off engineering workers, lost
In the electronics revolution. Along the prom

They'd holidayed on in childhood, with exotic walking sticks,
History in Residence, they moved

In Sophoclean raincoats. People laughed
At a world still made from girders, an Iron Age

Of Queen Elizabeths, pea-soupers, footplates,
And huge black toilet cisterns named 'St Mungo'.

Kids zapped the videogames in big arcades
Opposite Arran. Local people found

New energy sources, poems didn't rhyme.
The Pharaohs' grandchildren's accents sounded to them

Wee hell-taught ploughmen's. In slow seafront caffs
They felt poststructuralism, tanged with salt.

PHOTONICS

We're a new technology, a system that weds
Lasers; no electronics; no gob-drops
Of glass fibre to be teased and spun; just conjugate-phasing
Turning constant signals into rings of light,
A burgh packed with brilliant marriages

Strong the way a towerblock in an earthquake zone
Rocks and quivers, floating erect
On its bed of underground gravels; we're making discoveries,
Simplifying, unbuckling at the waist,
Unbuttoning the two pearl buttons at your throat,

Till we lie where the Giant flung his shining Causeway
Over gaunt blue water into these small sweet hills;
We meet as clearly as two beams in a saltire
Bonded at the centre, having each
Come through all the R & D to run on light.

THE DALSWINTON ENLIGHTENMENT

Patrick Miller's first iron vessel, the world's
First steamship is swanning across Dalswinton Loch.
A landscape painter, Alexander Nasmyth
Perches on deck beside his good friend, Robert Burns.

It's a calm, clear morning. The painter will later invent
The compression rivet, and work out the axial arrangement
Between propeller and engine. The poet will write about the light
Of science dawning over Europe, remembering how

Cold sun struck Pat's boat that October day at Dalswinton
When the churning paddles articulated the loch
In triumphant metre, and the locals made some cracks
Almost as if they were watching a ship of fools.

'I came across these facts which, mixed with others . . .'
Thinking of Helensburgh, J. G. Frazer
Revises flayings and human sacrifice;
Abo of the Celtic Twilight, St Andrew Lang
Posts him a ten-page note on totemism
And a coloured fairy book – an Oxford man
From Selkirk, he translates Homer in his sleep.

'When you've lived here, even for a short time,
Samoa's a bit like Scotland – there's the sea . . .
Back in Auld Reekie with a pen that sputtered
I wrote my ballad, "Ticonderoga" or
"A Legend of the West Highlands", then returned
To King Kalakaua's beach and torches –
You know my grandfather lit Lismore's south end?'

Mr Carnegie has bought Skibo Castle.
His union jack's sewn to the stars and stripes.
James Murray combs the dialect from his beard
And files slips for his massive *Dictionary*.
Closing a fine biography of mother,
Remembering Dumfries, and liking boys,
James Barrie, caught in pregnant London silence,
Begins to conceive the Never Never Land.

JOHN LOGIE BAIRD

When it rained past Dumbarton Rock
You skipped Classics for a motorbike exploration

Of the Clyde's slow Raj. In sodden memsahibs' gardens
Hydrangeas unfurled into fibre-optics.

A dominie lochgellied you once
For pronouncing 'Eelensburgh' like those wild, untouchable tinks

Who, if they could see your biker's career from today's
Long distance, would snigger. A socialist most famous for

Inventing an undersock, screened from douce cousins,
Under bamboos at a small jam factory

Near Port of Spain you achieved television
And paid for it. At the trials a boy called Reith

Risen from your old class shook hands, then wrote you off.
You worked. When World War II ended

Baird equipment broadcast victory in the Savoy
But not one diner said cheerio when you faded,

An obsolete wallah, edited out, still beaming
One hand outstretched across those Clydelike waves.

SYROPHENICIAN

You were the Syrophenician woman
Arguing with God, a dog among the Jews.
Glare islanded and baked you, shadows turned

On your crazy daughter. Border squatter
Between yes and no, you persisted, stubborn bitch
Till your answer ripened, like the nod to Zacchaeus in his tree

Or Loch Lomond light stunning a houseboat's windows
Into juddery polythene, a whiteout moment
When the one whom you loved most was healed.

INNER GLASGOW

You were a small red coat among the pit bings
That aren't there now, between Cambuslang
And Shettleston, with *Tell Me Why, Look and Learn*;

The quays have altered, liners replaced by jasmine;
Where docks are cultivated, hard nostalgia
Steam-rivets us to ghosts we love, in murals

Where everybody looks the same and sings
Of oppression, smokes, drinks lager, shouts out 'fuck'.
Shops sell us. Entrepreneurs' industrial

Museums postcard grime; we're pseudo-Griersonned.
But you refuse these foisted images, stay
Too true, still here, grown up in your red coat.

My inner Glasgow, you don't leave me, I
Do not leave you. A tubular steel frontage, roadcones
Flash towards us like the tiny folded pictures

In pop-up books, the lovely, lovely details
Too close to label art, that bring on laughter
When words cut out their starter motor, leaving us

Idling beside a cloudless firth. Those shorelights
Spread beyond Millport, beckon us to marry,
To lie along the bowsprits of our lives.

A SAYING

I'm calling you late in the evening, calling
Over hundreds of miles, you cannot hear me yet.

I'm calling you by a public name, a number;
Pushing the buttons. Roundabouts will be lit

By East Kilbride headlights, Polo Mint City they call it
Familiarly spinning its human rings of cars.

Through the machine I hear your Glasgow accent,
Your voiceprint. I just called, to say.

CAMBUSLANG

My childhood passes on a bicycle
Down West Coats Road, beneath our sycamore
That filters July sunlight through the slow
Sidereal quiet of the suburb

Where my father calls our garden 'the croft', and grows
Rows of potatoes, a countryman Glasgow disguised
Too long as a bank teller. A piece of broken glass
Shines on the lawn. Something always glistens

In the yards of grass that gently separate
A small boy from this same house where my parents
Live on together, smiling just beyond
The flowers-only gardens, the conservation area.

THE APPROACH

Floating, floating. In the tall dairy
Of the floods beyond, ruled with a grid of days,
Pigeons call. You remain like honey
Approaching through the hinterland, with deer abrupt
In front of the headlamps. You can absorb
Long novels of sleep and thermocouples
As the waves crash in. Night lowers its landing gear
And turns on one side. Over the telephone
Yesterday may be recounted.
Evening brindles, waiting outside the church
Pine smells blend with the scent of cooked food.
What time is it? Like oystercatchers, breath
On the flutehole quickens us, makes us persist;
It is approaching in boatsongs, it is approaching
With loyalty running in new shoes
Through a soaking meadow, pollen-drift
Sloughed off on your bare knees.
Each of us has the laser on the disc's rotation
Dispensing arias, zither's, moon-shaped lute's.
Feathered with a tang of salt, it approaches
Floating, about to be:
Ours, when the time is proper, silent
At the sea's edge, and the surf breeze brings you
Laughing ashore from the Gulf Stream at Machrihanish.

KYOTO

The peats stagger over the long brown cut. June
So hot that blue horses
Drift from the stained glass into the loch, Rannoch Moor
Hard as concrete. The ferry goes back and forward
Like a few simple cards reshuffled.
Crossing to the island, dragged through green water, crossing back.
90 in the shade. The longest day.
You could see to Kyoto
If you leant your head on my elbow.

NEC TAMEN CONSUMEBATUR

The most famous violinist on Eigg,
Denounced from the pulpit for his Gaelic folksongs,

Threw on the fire an instrument made
By a pupil of Stradivarius.

'The sooner,' thundered *The Times*,
'All Welsh specialities disappear

From the face of the earth the better.'
You whose parents came from a valley

North of Hanoi are now living in Princeton
Teaching low-temperature physics. Often

When you spoke about poems in Vietnamese
I heard behind the pride in your voice

Like a ceilidh in an unexpected place
The burning violins of small peoples.

MR AND MRS WILLIAM MULOCK
IN THE MUSEUM OF ETHNOLOGY

Mr Mulock, staring at
The gaps between the hieroglyphs,
Shuffles his feet, and wonders what
His wife sees in that row of stiffs

Embalmed in old stone coffins. She
Is rapturous, 'The guide book said,
"All visitors must go and see
The fertile Nile's immortal dead"

And now we have.' The husband coughs
But smiles to please his cultured wife;
Lost in the Pharaohs' autographs,
She disregards a common life.

Woman and man, each stands and seems
Odd, undeciphered, quite alone,
Surrounded by elusive dreams,
Fragments of the Rosetta Stone.

SCOTLAND

Glebe of water, country of thighs and watermelons
In seeded red slices, bitten by a firthline edged
With colonies of skypointing gannets,
You run like fresh paint under August rain.

It is you I return to, mouth of erotic Carnoustie,
Edinburgh in helio. I pass like an insect
Among shoots of ferns, gloved with pollen, intent
On listing your meadows, your pastoral Ayrshires, your glens

Gridded with light. A whey of meeting
Showers itself through us, sluiced from defensive umbrellas.
Running its way down raincoat linings, it beads
Soft skin beneath. A downpour takes us

At the height of summer, and when it is finished
Bell heather shines to the roots,
Belly-clouds cover the bings and slate cliffs,
Intimate grasses blur with August rain.

SCOTLAND

Semiconductor country, land crammed with intimate expanses,
Your cities are superlattices, heterojunctive
Graphed from the air, your cropmarked farmlands
Are epitaxies of tweed.

All night motorways carry your signal, swept
To East Kilbride or Dunfermline. A brightness off low headlands
Beams-in the dawn to Fife's interstices,
Optoelectronics of hay.

Micro-nation. So small you cannot be forgotten,
Bible inscribed on a ricegrain, hi-tech's key
Locked into the earth, your televised Glasgows
Are broadcast in Rio. Among circuitboard crowsteps

To be miniaturised is not small-minded.
To love you needs more details than the Book of Kells –
Your harbours, your photography, your democratic intellect
Still boundless, chip of a nation.

A SCOTTISH ASSEMBLY

Circuitry's electronic tartan, the sea,
Libraries, fields – I want the lot

To fly off and scatter, but most of all
Always to come home to roost

In this unkempt country where a handicapped printer,
Engraver of dog collars, began with his friends

The ultimate encyclopedia.
Don't expect any rhyme or reason

For Scotland remaining an explosion reversed
Or ordinariness a fruited vine

Or why I came back here to choose my union
On the side of the ayes, remaining a part

Of this diverse assembly – Benbecula, Glasgow, Bow of Fife –
Voting with my feet, and this hand.

EDINBURGH

My capital of sulking jewels
Misinvested, glimmers through the haar.
Under it, horsehair sofas, quaichs
And portrait heads in museum store-tunnels
Furnish the salons of an independent
Doppelgänger-townscape, locked.

Above ground, councillors start to debate
Charging admission to the city.
An occasional tubelit attendant
Visits that undernation where every item
Has its provenance label, an accurate pawnticket
Ready in case of redemption.

SIR DAVID BREWSTER INVENTS
THE KALEIDOSCOPE

He clears the atmosphere of cool St Andrews –
Into dense constellations that revolve
At a hand's turn. From Aberdeen, Lord Byron
Looks on with half of Europe, starry-eyed.
Baudelaire will say modern art's like this,
Brilliant and shifty, a fantastic model
Of how the real will open up, the micro-
Particular, the split, then the expanding
Universe that spills out silent stars
Light years from Scotland. It's a toy –
No copyright, it made the man who made it
No money. Just a universal sold
In Glasgow or Bangkok. With an English friend
Later he helped invent the camera,
Became a friend of Hill and Adamson
Who set up tripods in Fife villages,
Went back to being local, became fact.

BEDROOM

Across the firth at dusk from the Kilmacolm road
Come stalks of light. The one bank touches the other.
A mica evening. Greenock signals across

To a window high on the Hill House. Instead of curtains
White wooden shutters ready to be fastened

Going to bed. That room's a museum now
Pale with chinoiserie beyond the harling.
Nobody dreams there. Everybody does.

RAIN

A motorbike breaks down near Sanna in torrential rain,
Pouring loud enough to perforate limousines, long enough
To wash us to Belize. Partick's
Fish-scaled with wetness. Drips shower from foliage, cobbles, tourists
From New York and Düsseldorf at the tideline
Shoes lost in bogs, soaked in potholes, clarted with glaur.
An old woman is splashed by a bus. A gash
In cloud. Indians
Arrived this week to join their families and who do not feel
Scottish one inch push onwards into a drizzle
That gets heavy and vertical. Golf umbrellas
Come up like orchids on fast-forward film; exotic
Cagoules fluoresce nowhere, speckling a hillside, and

                                        plump

Off dykes and gutters, overflowing
Ditches, a granary of water drenches the shoulders
Of Goatfell and Schiehallion. Maps under perspex go bleary,
Spectacles clog, Strathclyde, Tayside, Dundee
Catch it, fingers spilling with water, oil-stained
As it comes down in sheets, blows
Where there are no trees, snow-wet, without thought of the morrow.
Weddings, prunes, abattoirs, strippers, Glen Nevis, snails
Blur in its democracy, down your back, on your breasts.
In Kilmarnock a child walks naked. A woman laughs.
In cars, in Tiree bedrooms, in caravans and tenements,
Couples sleeved in love, the gibbous Govan rain.

ALBA EINSTEIN

When proof of Einstein's Glaswegian birth
First hit the media everything else was dropped:
Logie Baird, Dundee painters, David Hume – all
Got the big E. Physics documentaries
Became peak-viewing; Scots publishers hurled awa
MacDiarmid like an overbaked potato, and swooped
On the memorabilia: *Einstein Used My Fruitshop*,
Einstein in Old Postcards, Einstein's Bearsden Relatives.
Hot on their heels came the A. E. Fun Park,
Quantum Court, Glen Einstein Highland Malt.
Glasgow was booming. Scotland rose to its feet
At Albert Suppers where The Toast to the General Theory
Was given by footballers, panto-dames, or restaurateurs.
In the US an ageing lab-technician recorded
How the Great Man when excited showed a telltale glottal stop.
He'd loved fiddlers' rallies. His favourite sport was curling.
Thanks to this, Scottish business expanded
Endlessly. His head grew toby-jug-shaped,
Ideal for keyrings. He'd always worn brogues.
Ate bannocks in exile. As a wee boy he'd read *The Beano*.
His name brought new energy: our culture was solidly based
On pride in our hero, The Universal Scot.

THE SCOTTISH NATIONAL
CUSHION SURVEY

Our heritage of Scottish cushions is dying.
Teams of careful young people on training schemes
Arrived through a government incentive, counting
Every cushion. In Saltcoats, through frosty Lanark.
They even searched round Callanish
For any they'd missed. There are no more Scottish cushions
Lamented the papers. Photographs appeared
Of the last cushion found in Gaeldom.
Silk cushions, pin cushions, pulpit cushions.
We must preserve our inheritance.
So the museums were built: The Palace of Cushions, the National
Museum of Soft Seating, and life went on elsewhere
Outside Scotland. The final Addendum was published
Of *Omnes Pulvini Caledonii.*
Drama documentaries. A chapter closed.
And silently in Glasgow quick hands began
Angrily making cushions.

AH WAANT

Ah waant yon guid aucht that's weet as olours, rerr
As spluntin acors thi Mojave – mair thumblickin,
Prollin thumbs hurry burry aw owre yi, wi nae
Hurkle-durkle; stramash o reists an shanks,

Loup ourweillin inventars o loo:
Loofs, lonyngs, skirdoch o orising, red.
An mornin a poddasway ayont thi hairst-rig,
A souple, souple dawn.

*I want that good intimate possession that's wet as herbs liked by
swans, rare as running after girls at night across the Mojave –
more making of bargains by licking thumbs, licking and striking
thumbs in confused hurry all over you, with no sluggishness in
bed; disturbance of restive waiting insteps and legs, leap exceed-
ing inventories of love: palms of the hand, narrow passageways,
flirting of arising, spawning place. And morning a garment
whose warp and woof are silk, beyond the couple who reap
together at harvest, a supple, cunning dawn.*

DAY COWPS

Day cowps, swaagin,
Simmer-flaws pasperin thi milkmaid's path
Whan thi pap o thi hass, eefauld as a rock-doo,
Shaks sangs ayont thi earny-couligs.

In yon king's weathir Ah tak yir haun
By thi pirliewinkie an get yi up tae thi taing.
Oor boadies mell lik thi raise-net fishin,
Lik a kindlie tae Adam's wine.

*Day spills over, fluttering like a bird's wing, ground mists that rise
from the soil on a hot day turning the Milky Way to samphires,
when the uvula, honest as a wild pigeon, shakes songs beyond the
tumuli. In these exhalations rising from the earth on a warm day
I take your hand by the smallest finger and go with you up to the
headland. Our bodies grow intimate like that kind of fishing
where part of the net rises and flows and subsides with the tide,
like an ancestral claim to water.*

CHEVALIER

The voice is holed up in a cave. Water drips on it. Silent,
Despised men keep watch outside.

The voice in the heather, disguised as a woman, moves
Mostly at night. Money's available

For information about the voice. Vessels
Wait all day offshore, listening.

The voice is nearly inaudible on a tiny island. Sun beats
    down on its vowels.
People are burned out for the voice, which sheds

Enough clothes for many generations. They festoon museums.
It gets so quiet searchers hear nothing,

Can't even tell its language. The voice escapes
To Argentina and Cape Breton Island, gets drunk,

Mouthing obscenities, toasting itself
Over and over. Silence doesn't chasten it.

Rewards and spies increase. The voice
Loses consciousness, won't be betrayed.

SIMULTANEOUS TRANSLATION

It fills up the pause when you finish speaking,
Or even before you've stopped,

Gets between the chewy biro and the word-processor,
Between 'Yours sincerely' and your name.

Other times you walk right into it
At Aberfeldy, going over the Highland Line

Towards something you can't understand,
Also somewhere you've been.

Gaels in Glasgow, Bangladeshis in Bradford,
Negotiators, opera-buffs, tourists:

This is where we all live now,
Wearing something like a Sony Walkman,

Hearing another voice every time we speak.
A girl opens her mouth and an Oxbridge bass

Is talking in English. What is she really saying?
Already her finger is starting to creep

Closer to the binding of a parallel text,
Between the lines, then crossing over.

STASH

To know is to slip your hand inside
A secret place, and close on the roundness of glass,

The neck of a bottle in its darkened niche,
An unsmashed Reformation saint.

To know is to detect
Telltale signs: stains, wheeltracks,

Smeek of rich, spirituous fires,
Vestiges of creation.

★

Outsiders come to trap that knowledge,
Bearing down on the spirit's vessels

With the weight of the law, but the makers are too light-footed.
They gather up their gleaming test-tubes,

Camouflage fires, cram their bottles
Down rock-fissures too remote and obstinate

For the hands of the Revenue to reach between roots.
A slow, patient, moony Resistance

Lies in wait for the throats of children,
Ready to rage and confer its blessing

That till now is illicit and still.

MARY OF BERNERA

Mary of Bernera, doe-eyed Mary, Mary of the songs, you are as honey and your breasts are as sweet white apples, but I no longer find you erotically attractive. When the Minister of the Free Church preached his sermon against my hands inside your bathing dress I was in the kirk and was traumatized by it. All the energies which our love consumed I now devote to marketing edible seaweeds. Mary of Bernera, doe-eyed Mary, Mary of the songs, though I cannot be with you I have your eyelashes in a small box. I carry it with me to the sea's edge and on the shingle. I who was your lover now sell seaweed to old crofters from a Renault van. There is a matchbox in my overalls. Think on me, Mary of the songs.

RADIO SCOTTISH DEMOCRACY

You hear an old man scratching himself
Before he gets up at Kinlochmoidart.

You tune in to a woman in Lima, yawning.
You listen to what hasn't happened yet, the shout

That is still just an intake of breath;
Straining so hard, your imagination

Becomes a microphone for the future.
A new voice starts to come unjammed

Against a rout of white-noise, Floddens,
Cullodens, nostalgias that rhyme,

When kilties went roaring over the grass,
Fell on it, let it grow through them.

You pick up words moving – towards or away?
Reaction times quicken. Is that it? Listen –

Not to dour centuries of trudging,
Marching, and taking orders;

Today I have heard the feet of my country
Breaking into a run.

PRAYER

Upstream from shattered urban lintels
Lost crofts are soft as new bread.

That dripping tap in the one-walled kitchen
Reminds someone there will be a need
Of water before and after.

Sin to imagine a perfect world
Without embarrassment, rain, or prayer.
A hand is clasping my other hand

In a dark place that has to be got through
On a wing and. Listen to this.

BOY

My left hand is turning into a herring.
The fingers I write with get doughy

So it hurts to shake hands – feels as if
People tear at my fingers like rolls.

I want to greet them with my left. They shun it
Because it has a briny smell,

But out here in a strange place I'm learning
To cope with offering both hands

To the sitting crowd. When they grip me, each man and woman
Seems full. This

Must be the meaning of shaking hands
With five thousand people. They're rising,

Fed, leaving the bowl of the hills
Strewn with left-overs, me among them.

Everybody's gone now. I'm just thirteen.
I understand I don't understand it.

MC

'Going to hell in a hurry. Send *The Wykehamist*'.
1916, awarded Military Cross.

MA, BD. At Nakusp, BC,
Preaches to thumbless lumberjacks. Takes tea at Harvard.

New charge – galvanic Pope of Govan –
Unemployed and Iona Abbey

Rebuild one another as ordered.
World War Two: 'I am a man

With a jammed Bren gun, but not so jammed.
I hit with one bullet in five.'

Old age, psoriasis: put feet in poly bags.
Tell Duke of Edinburgh: BAN THE BOMB.

Immersion

In mud, weeds, leaves, preaching
Christ of Ecology at Morven, car converted

To diesel in the 70s. Public weeping when wife dies,
Wrinkles in the age of the image.

We Shall Rebuild. Iona rebuilt.
We Shall Rebuild. Yells: 'I have maintained

This single-minded passion for so many years
By being deaf.' Military. Cross.

ABERDEENSHIRE

Oilrig excaliburs of burning gas,
Sheep coughing through a starlit igloo silence
Near Craigievar, the reeling of dancers

Spattering an on-off wind's signal
Broken up by granite and salmon,
Whitewater *bon viveurs*.

The King's College corona satellite-tracks
Star dialects. Hills budge
And settle. Grouse flurry. Computer screens dazzle the night,
Their flickering eyes added to the land's.

BOND

In his late eighties he still took his dog to the cinema. They went to see *You Only Live Twice*. His daughter-in-law would get very embarrassed; 'someone's got to sit on that seat afterwards.' Ears cocked, the collie perched on the velour. A man in the row behind leant forward, gave a tap on the shoulder. 'Hey, mister, is yur dug enjoyin the pictchur?' 'Aye, son, can ye no tell? He's seen all the James Bonds. He feels it's a shame it's no still Sean Connery but.'

THE HUMANITY CLASSROOM

Sitting there, I was a comma in the bible;
On either side great generations of talk.

The word means Latin. Stubbornly at the Uni
They went on calling it Humanity.

Before my time, in mid-*Aeneid*
A woman at the lectern under big oil portraits

Threw open a window, leaned out listening
To riveters at work in the shipyards.

THE GLASGOW HERALD

On industrial evenings serenaded by welding
At Colville's Steelworks, one white-hot pouring arc
Glimpsed from a diesel, I carried my paintings in a plastic sack

Through Central Station, hearing the woman announcer
Calling Ardrossan, Polmadie, Haymarket, Pollokshaws, a
   random timetable
Rich as Los Angeles, New York with bracken and grass.

Her messages in the middle Sixties
Still held a departing tremor of steam, the Greenock
Blitz, torpedoes on wagons, my parents' threatened

Destinations. At Dalmarnock Power Station the sky enlarged
Over and over, above towerblocks, beyond the Campsies
Brushed by works hooters, the lyric blasts of a train.

AT LANSDOWNE KIRK

You see from gold-leaf behind the pulpit
Between the years 1914 and '19
McNeil was not a good name to have.

'*I am the true Vine.*' In plaster relief
Behind St Andrew, St Margaret, St Mungo
 Are kneeling killers – Wallace, and Robert the Bruce

With the words 'Death or Liberty' at his ear.
The bare toes of Christ's right foot
Peep from his robe. Round him

The only figure in modern dress
Is a kilted soldier, kneeling with fixed bayonet.
Seventy years after the Armistice

He is still holding, still laying down his gun.

FIANCÉE

She reads by gas. Their engagement will be as long
As her mother's illness. A motor car splashes on the cobbles.

Each Christmas they exchange poets
In the padded leather bindings that will soon go out of fashion.

She glides upstairs, carrying fresh linen.
Mother walks to the toilet. Clouds are banked over the Firth.

In his photograph he is wearing a starched wing-collar.
They initial their endpapers, adding the date:

'07, '08, '09.
Upstairs is quiet. She sits in the parlour

Patiently reading, '*I am very dreary,*
He will not come', she said.

LOVE POEM FOR ALICE
WITH OLD CARS

In the new dream I give you a big-radiatored
100-miles-on-a-gallon-of-water steamcar
Exported by the White Sewing Machine Co.,
Cleveland, Ohio. You scoot with aplomb

Through Alexandria to Loch Lomond past the indigenous
Argyll Motors Factory with its built-to-last
Stone car over the door. People call you odd,
Determined, unchaperoned, 'fast'. Your wheels cover

Scotland, familiar and intimate, Tin-Lizzying
Right up Ben Nevis, mass-produced,
Laughing with the dash of the woman driver's
TS1, first car in Dundee. Your fingers

Run through my hair in the rain with the uniqueness
Of Tullock's 1910 St Magnus
Handmade on mainland Orkney. A crowd of boys in caps
Skips beside us, mouthing

Names of shared loves: Arrol Johnston,
Delaunay-Belleville, Renault. A twine of exhaust
Ties up the Pass of Brander. Can the greenhouse effect
Scrub out this joyful woman driver

Insouciant at the wheel of a Detroit-built Hudson, her glance
Thrown devil-may-caringly through its rear window,
Male passenger, watching her high heel pushing eagerly
Up away into the hills?

ANNE OF GREEN GABLES

Short moneyless summers at West Kilbride you sat out
On the back steps with a view of the outside toilet
Reading the Anne books, one after the datestamped next,

Anne of Windy Willows, Anne of Avonlea,
Anne of the Island, Anne's House of Dreams.
No books were ever as good as these

From West Kilbride Public Library
That always had to go back.
When we got married, one by one

You bought the whole set, reading them through. At first
I was jealous when you sat not speaking,
Then put the books away on your own shelf.

'"How white the moonlight is tonight," said Anne
Blythe to herself.' At first
I was jealous. Not now.

NORTH-EAST FIFE

You are the instrument
Generations have played on

Under the fields of Crail and Anstruther
Combs and mirrors in an Aero-bar darkness

After the Picts, small stone churches
Outlived cathedrals as a tin whistle outlasts an organ.

You are the true postmodern script
Whose every letter is robbed from an earlier writing,

Unkirkcaldied, Dundeeless, smug,
Too full of your earlier selves,

Sunlit evenings' bohemian fishertowns,
Home of the avant-golf,

In between the high-summer fields
Identities spilling like wisps of hay

Blown from the back of a horse-drawn cart
That is slowly becoming a tractor.

A QUIET MAN

My best friend at school, then at university
Turned out to be gay

Which was fine, but left me somehow
Lonely. I knew I'd never

Be a ladies' man, or a man's man either.
Unpubby, hating cigarette smoke,

I took out girls to the Art Galleries,
Typing them sonnets. I mooned,

Living in fear some reintroduced
National Service sergeant major

Would noisily break me in two.
Odd those sergeant majors now

Are gender fossils, and here I am
Washing the dishes but not doing ironing,

Married. Evolved from my all-male school
And that bristling, women-only college

I lived in later for years,
I stand off-balance, mumbling something

About our wee son's future, his stripy flag
A dishtowel my Dad brandished when he made me

Like him an in-between, quiet man,
Homo silens, a missing link.

CHAPS

With his Bible, his Burns, his brose and his baps,
Colonel John Buchan is one of the chaps,
With his mother, his mowser, his mauser, his maps,
Winston S. Churchill is one of the chaps.

CHAPS   CHAPS   CHAPS   CHAPS
CHAPS   CHAPS   CHAPS   CHAPS

Rebecca Mphalele is one of the chaps,
Ezekiel Ng is one of the chaps,
Queenie Macfadzean is one of the chaps,
Kayode Nimgaonkar is one of the chaps.

CHAPS   CHAPS   CHAPS   CHAPS
CHAPS   CHAPS   CHAPS   CHAPS

Oxfordy chaps, Cambridgey chaps,
Glasgowy chaps, Harrovian chaps,
Oxfordy chaps, Cambridgey chaps,
Oxfordy chaps, Cambridgey chaps.

CHAPS   CHAPS   CHAPS   CHAPS
CHAPS   CHAPS   CHAPS   CHAPS

The sergeant's a chap, the rifle's a chap,
The veldt is a chap, the heather's a chap,
A great JCR of them tossing their caps
Like schoolboys at Eton dyed red on the maps.

CHAPS   CHAPS   CHAPS   CHAPS
CHAPS   CHAPS   CHAPS   CHAPS

The porthole's a chap, the cannon's a chap,
The Haigs and the Slessors, the Parks are all chaps,
Mungos and Maries, filling the gaps
In the Empire's red line that can never collapse.

CHAPS   CHAPS   CHAPS   CHAPS
CHAPS   CHAPS   CHAPS   CHAPS

Lord Kitchener needs them to pose for his snaps
Of Ypres and Verdun with chaps' heads in their laps
Singing Gilbert and Sullivan or outlining traps
To catch rowdies at Eights Week, next year perhaps.

CHAPS   CHAPS   CHAPS   CHAPS
CHAPS   CHAPS   CHAPS   CHAPS

The war memorial's a chap, the codebook's a chap,
The wind is a chap, the horse is a chap,
The knitters, the padres, the limbs are all chaps
From Hawick and Africa, poppies are chaps

CHAPS   CHAPS   CHAPS   CHAPS
CHAPS   CHAPS   CHAPS   CHAPS

MENDING THE HELICOPTER

I'm too busy mending the helicopter
To wash up yesterday's dishes.

I'm too busy mending the helicopter
To pick up the kids from school.

I'm too busy mending the helicopter
To talk to your doctor about my cigarettes.

I'm too busy mending the helicopter.
I'll have to work through the night with arc lights.

Who do you think I'm mending this helicopter *for*?

Reply

I've already mended the helicopter.
Leave those rotorblade sprockets alone.

I've already mended the helicopter
While you were watching *Apocalypse Now*.

I've already mended the helicopter.
It needed mending. Radar was a terrible mess.

I've already mended the helicopter.
Why are you out there at night on the lawn

Taking the whole thing to bits?

MALE INFERTILITY

Slouched there in the Aston Martin
On its abattoir of upholstery

He escapes
To the storming of the undersea missile silo,

The satellite rescue, the hydrofoil
That hits the beach, becoming a car

With Q's amazing state-of-the-art,
State-of-the-art, state-of-the-art . . .

Suddenly he has this vision
Of a sperm in a boyhood sex-ed film

As a speargun-carrying, tadpole-flippered frogman
Whose visor fills up with tears,

And of living forever in a dinnerjacket,
Fussier and fussier about what to drink,

Always, 'Shaken, not stirred.'
Chlorine-blue bikinis, roulette tables, waterskiing –

Show me that scene in *Thunderball*
Where James Bond changes a nappy.

RIPENING

My mother buys my dad a new tweed jacket
Very rarely, always at the sales.

Upstairs in one of two mahogany wardrobes
He hangs it like a shot bird to be cured,

New for a decade, it takes on the smell
Of jackets round it, his scent, the reek of mothballs.

On coathangers, suspended in the dark,
Herringbone accepts the gift of waiting.

Unseasoned pockets sense how ripened pockets
Unfold receipts and stones, then yield up string.

As they get worn, my mother schools thinned elbows
In leather patches, and younger jackets learn

To renounce fashion long before he wears them.
'Is that a new jacket?' 'Yes,' he says, 'it is.'

US

Silence parked there like a limousine;
We had no garage and we had no car.

Dad polished shoes, boiled kettles for hot-water bottles,
And mother made pancakes, casseroles, lentil soup

On her New World cooker, its blue and cream
Obsolete before I was born.

I was a late, only child, campaigning
For 33 r.p.m. records.

Dad brought food parcels from City Bakeries
In crisp brown paper, tightly bound with string.

So many times he felt annoyed
When a visitor left without shutting the gate.

Now someone will bid for, then clear these rooms,
Stripping them of us. We were that floral wallpaper,

That stuck serving-hatch, radiograms polished and broken,
Dogeared carpet-tiles that understood us,

Our locked bureau, crammed with ourselves.

BOVRILISM

Tramping around as a corduroy student
I was always about to begin The Next Movement in Art.

True, my paintings were pretty sub-
The Scottish Colourists of the 1920s,

But, excitingly, in that dragged brushstroke
Or that stipple, I could see the point

From which in my next-but-one canvas
A new departure might depart.

Now I concentrate on mortgagism,
Dabbling a bit in tinted stuff

Whose varnishy, soulful burnt umbers
Seem somehow, well, *bovriliste*.

THE UMBRELLA STAND

The eroticism of hand-knitted cardigans,
Shower caps and overshoes, wee earthenware pigs
Just to take the chill off the sheets

Dogs me: endearments of freely given
Potatoes and turnips, summer fruits,
Heinz 57, Milk Tray.

Sex was changing in a neuk in the rocks
Carefully into a one-piece bathing suit
On the edge of a cool, sunny ocean.

Sometimes at my parents' house I search
For that alert, tweed-flecky light in their eyes
Through which I came to exist.

SCOTCH BROTH

A soup so thick you could shake its hand
And stroll with it before dinner.

The face rising to its surface,
A rayfish waiting to be stroked,

Is the pustular, eat-me face of a crofter,
Turnipocephalic, white-haired.

Accepting all comers, it's still our nation's
Flagsoup, sip-soup; sip, sip, sip

At this other scotch made with mutton
That intoxicates only

With peas and potatoes, chewy uists of meat.
All races breathe over our bowl,

Inhaling Inverness and Rutherglen,
Waiting for a big, teuchtery face

To compose itself from carrots and barley
Rising up towards the spoon.

RECALL

I have recalled the Scottish Parliament
From hatbands and inlaid drawers,

From glazed insides of earthenware teapots,
Corners of greenhouses, tumblers

Where it has lain in session too long,
Not defunct but slurring its speeches

In a bleary, irresolute tirade
Affronting the dignity of the house,

Or else exiled to public transport
For late-night sittings, the trauchled members

Slumped in wee rows either side of the chamber
Girning on home through the rain.

My aunt died, waiting for this recall
In her Balfron cottage. I want her portrait

Hung with those of thousands of others
Who whistled the auld sang toothily under their breath.

Let her be painted full-length, upright
In her anorak, flourishing secateurs.

She knew the MPs in funny wigs
Would return bareheaded after their long recess

To relearn and slowly unlearn themselves,
Walking as if in boyhood and girlhood

They'd just nipped down to the shops for the messages
And taken the winding path back.

THE CELTIC SAINTS

One twirls a shamrock to explain the Trinity, another
Exorcises a sea-serpent;

Coracling everywhere, spinning round
In their offshore dodgems, banging into gales

Near Lismore or Greenland, birled like Celtic knots,
Their journeys are doodled by God, pushing out

From the Hebrides of themselves – their cells
Made of strong skin, like the body

Avoiding the devil, singing endlessly
Into the endless, praising running water

For its non-stop; their medieval Latin
Is light and hymnlike, a Pictish whisper

Taking the form of an Irish wolfhound
That courses the hills from another mirrory loch

Still undiscovered, with its small green island, its ringing
Bronze quadrangular bell.

JESUS CHRIST ENDORSES THE NEW HILLMAN IMP

I was in our works canteen when a call
Came over the tannoy to watch him endorse the new car.
As he bent and touched it, he said,
'This product will save your area
For another decade: it will be loved
Equally by US management
And families whom its air-cooled rear engine
Will power to school. I'm saying this
That you may take pride in your work.'
Nervous execs whooshed him away
For a photo session.
                           I lost my job
In the first redundancies.
'Does the daffodil have an income allocation model?
Will the company keep you safe
In a world downturn? Will you see this factory levelled?'
Hillmans have long gone out of production.
My launch brochures in a box upstairs
With his photo are greeny with damp.
We did good work, though. No regrets.
It was true what he said, standing up
On a platform in Linwood, Scotland,
Endorsing the new Hillman Imp.

THE NUMTIES

The parsnip Numties: I was a teenager then,
Collecting clip-together models
Of historical windsocks, dancing the Cumbernauld bump.

Satirical pornography, plant-staplers, nostalgiaform shoes
Were brochure-fresh. It was numty-four
I first saw a neighbour laughing in a herbal shirt.

Moshtensky, Garvin, Manda Sharry –
Names as quintessentially Numties
As Hearers and Bonders, duckponding, or getting a job

In eradication. Everything so familiar and sandwiched
Between the pre-Numties and the debouch of decades after.
I keep plunging down to the wreck

Of the submerged Numties, every year
Bringing back something jubilantly pristine,
Deeper drowned, clutching my breath.

LA MER

Is that a bathing cap or a seal's head
Surfacing in the 1930s?

This morning the sea does a huge baking
Of scones and fresh apple tart,

Mixed up with herring, cod and shrimps,
Cuttlefish, fruits de mer.

The sea clears everything away
To set a fresh place. It repeats itself

Like Alzheimer's Disease.
Its moony rollers cast me ashore –

A creel, a fishbox from Crail or Vilnius,
A piece of boat, old but ready

To be put to some startling re-use.
Voices, phonelines, everything flows:

Dad in his landing-craft, beached
At Normandy, us cruising the Small Isles

In the Seventies, Eigg, Rhum, Muck, Canna
Bobbing up one by one, dark collies

 Chasing their tails, retrieving sticks from the breakers,
Mr McConnochie's painting of Aphrodite

Breezing to the Arisaig beach on a clamshell.
When I was wee I knew the music

Was about the sea, but I thought its title
Was a French phrase meaning 'My Mother'.

WINTER

That night we drove to hear about adoption
You jumped an unmarked junction, trying to find
The Social Work Centre. When we did, we sat
Ten minutes in the warm car, then went in.

We were the quietest of all the couples.
The walls were covered in felt-pen drawings, toys
Cluttered the place. Committedly,
A foster-parent told us what that meant

But cold seeped in from black-iced Dundee streets;
Swing-doors blew open; if it snowed, they'd close the bridge,
Stranding us there. I couldn't really tell
Just what we wanted. I wanted too much:

Not to feel so old, to be able to believe in luck,
To remember sitting with these other couples
In a semi-circle on bright scatter-cushions
Watching a vid in coats and anoraks.

SEAHORSES

At night they fly up from the road's
Cat's-eyes, two fresh splashes of seaweed,

A lovely omen, intertwined
Round the farmtouns of Angus, throwing the North Sea in the air,

Floating us deeper into our marriage
With fins and wings, bucking hooves rapping

Horse against horse in eared darkness,
You-me and I-you, there ahead

The dancing seahorses of Aberlemno
Sheheing upright along the night,

Wee dragons, sheltie-haddocks, curled
Round one another, eye to eye,

Take us up into the Angus evening,
Take us up, then plunge us under.

THE HANDSHAKES

I flinched at the handshake of a woman in labour
Through mid-contraction when you pushed our son

Down towards the forceps.
Soon his fingers curled

Possessively around my index finger
And then round yours,

Welcoming us with a reflex action
To take your hand beyond yon Labour Suite

Where you clutched me as you breathed the Entonox
And called for your own mother, who is dead.

THE CRITICISM

I who can't play any instrument,
Whose singing is crap, who was once chucked out of a choir

For my utterly expressionless face,
Sing to my baby till his rubbed-at eyelids

Waver. He sprawls in my arms
Not knowing if he's hearing 'The Skye Boat Song',

'Silent Night' or some early Seventies
TV soundtrack. He falls asleep

With a whole-body look of ecstatic boredom,
His breathing in tune with my own.

THE JUDGE

At six months my son sits like a judge
On the High Chairage of Scotland.

His hands rest on a wee shelf in front of him.
He weighs us up. He takes advice from a spoon,

And we crouch, looking on, waiting
Years for a sentence that, when it comes,

Will be reported wise, long-considered,
Irreproachably just.

SOBIESKI-STUARTS

On scuffed chaise-longues in Europe's drawing-rooms
Sobieski-Stuarts audition for thrones.

Their Gaelic is not the Gaelic of Borrodale
But the Gaelic of Baden-Baden.

Draped in ancient, oddly pristine
Manic-depressive tartans,

Soi-distant with calipered wrists,
Statuesque for early cameras,

Soon they pirouette to receive
Double malts and weary autograph hunters,

Couples rubicundly stripping the willow
After the band has gone home.

Trains connect for the Hook of Holland,
Luxembourg, St Germain.

Underneath heavy evening cloud
The sun sets, a jabot of light.

THE DESCENT

(S.J.B., *1957–1995*)

Roped to myself, I inched away
Down towards a bottle-dungeon where
Dank slabs forgot the normal day.
Inside it, knotted with despair,

I laughed and told my cleverest jokes,
I told the best jokes, I was told
My bottle-dungeon was a hoax
I'd see through, if I just grew old.

Sometimes I am the Joycean face,
The cobbled street you drift along,
The video shop, the tashed briefcase,
The tenor breaking into song

In Gaelic or Italian, 'Oh!'
Stroke your baby in his cot,
His curls, his skin-folds that will grow
Smoothed out. I have to cut this knot.

THE RESULT

1707–1997; for Alice

Moments after death, I found my voice
Surprising, hearing my own

Ansafone saying, 'I'm not here just now,
Please speak after the tone.'

You saw it in my eyes – release
Back to the world. More, more

You, Scotland, sea, each lost and re-elected.
I toast debatable lands, the come-go shore

Of living here. 'Thanks!' My full, bannock-smeared glass
Rises to you, our son, and our new, blonde

Daughter. We dance, in grey St Michael slippers,
Cancerless, broken out, and passed beyond.

KNOWLEDGE

Ferrier invents the word *epistemology*
Sitting in a doorway wiped across with light

From an early flashgun. Round him, young buck students
Scatter in the aftershock, vanish.

★

Euclidean rain stots on cobbles
In wintry St Andrews. Ferrier hunches with cold,

Drawing his black gown over his head
Like a photographer, abolishing himself.

★

A sore has developed, a gland gone syphilitic.
He reads up the chemistry of mercuric oxide,

Hears his Aunt Susan, the famous author
Of *Marriage*, has died in her sleep.

★

Frail, he blocks a lecture-room entrance.
A New Woman confronts him: 'I wish to know

By what right you keep me from these Chemistry lectures.'
He can't move, at one with the stone.

PASSAGE

in memory of John Lorne Campbell and Margaret Fay Shaw

'Record me,' she laughs through her Gaelic dance-steps
While the cylinder reeling round and round
Scratches itself with song.

Old women's brittle notes are held
On nerve-thin, tautened Ediphone wire,
A longitude of music

Stretched in one unending passage
From the Isle of Canna to Nova Scotian
Tape-hiss of wind on snow

Where the gone-away, digitized pew by pew,
Climb aboard long tunes outlasting lips
Danced down into the machine.

BEREAVEMENT

I walk the same roads far ahead of you,
So slowly, but you never catch me up.

Your stick, homing from Market Street to South Street,
Takes you away a slightly different route.

I peer in windows at your lost reflection,
Catching you looking through me, out to sea.

We haunt each other, almost happily,
Until each sinks back into his real world,

Children dismounted from tonight's last train
At the wrong station, who can hear

Carriages that went ahead without them
Decades ago, still singing in the rails.

LAUGHING GIFTBALL

Yule-wrapped in its resilient, mucusine box,
Laughing Giftball puts the bounce into Christmas.

Ergonomic Giftball comes guaranteed
For four hundred hours of muscle-toning playtime;

Should you wish to profit from Giftball for longer,
Send it for checking to our Isle of Lewis factory.

For safety, keep Giftball away
From liquid helium, elderly persons, or water.

In some countries Giftball's fluorescent coating
Triggers treatable allergies. If in doubt, phone our free Skinline.

Thrown incorrectly, Giftball can emit a tone
Occasioning nausea and infrequent anal bleeding;

However, when propelled at the correct velocity,
Giftball will not shatter into shrapnel-like, lancing shards.

If your Giftball comes with the Giftball Xmas Launcher,
This must never be pointed at people, brickwork, or animals.

Should the Giftball's cap become detached
Evacuate the area. Giftball's patent core

Constitutes a powerful, recognized defoliant
(World copyright protected). Laughing Giftball

May interfere with pacemakers, satellites, and rechargeable shavers,
Should not be ingested, inverted, or retrieved by dogs.

Avoid indoor use. For more guidance see our website
aa dot aa dot rgh

Thank you for choosing Laughing Giftball.
Keep these instructions with you at all times.

IMPOSSIBILITY

Under the North Sea, a mile off Elie
Where once she was noticed in a mullioned window,
White lace cap rising, brooding over her table,
Margaret Oliphant Wilson Oliphant
Translates on to starfish and nacred shells
Montalembert's *Monks of the West*

Still weary, awash with hackwork to support
Dead Maggie, Marjorie, Tiddy, and Cecco,
Her water babies, breathing ectoplasm,
She watches aqualungs glow with shellac,
Mindful how she loves light's aftermath,
Protozoa's luminescent wash

On the Firth of Forth; she drifts
Eagerly shorewards, can almost touch
Piers at St Andrews, cybery, Chopinesque fingers
Of Tentsmuir Sands, Blackwood's Strathtyrum
Pressure-resistant, bathyscaphic den
Deeply upholstered with morocco books

Ich bin Margaret Oliphant
Je suis Margaret Oliphant
I am Margaret Oliphant
You are Margaret Oliphant
Vous êtes Margaret Oliphant
Sie sind Margaret Oliphant

I love my home, its *lares et penates*
Of broken shoe buckles, balls of green wool,
Needles, its improvisatory architecture
Feeding my work with interruptions, turns
Snatched, forty-winked; stashed seed pearls in a dish
Radiate homely, incarnational light

Sometimes the green walls glimmer, elverish,
Phosphorescent, spectrally alive,
Razorfish splay galvanized medium's fingers
Seeking burnished heads of polyps and carrageen
Brocaded with plankton, nuzzled by antlered snails,
Vulval, brasslit, flecked and veined and washed

Dinner-suited Auchterlonian clubmen
Fill the fishtank windows of the R & A;
Subsea, in my dark, Victorian
Antimacassared, embroidered sewing room,
I'm inky, threaded with spectra, gynaecological
Eyeball thistle-tassels of the sea

Brown, blue-grey, single-cell-like
Pre-embryo materials in store
But never used, spermatozoic spirits
Haunt the sunned waters, seances of plankton lie
Paperweight-still, flower heads, floating marbles
Undulating in slow liquid glass

I am too antisyzygously Scottish,
Thirled to names like Eden, Wallyford,
Pittenweem; tidally to and fro
Mights and maybes captivate me, I waver
Between hot toddy and hard, cold-boiled chuckies
Smooth and rounded as a baby's skull

Oceans teem with informational currents;
Lord Kelvin's submarine telegraphy
Nets continents; minke whales, prawns,
Mackerel and reef-life hover, agog
Though bored by its contents: same old same old
Verisimilitudinous whine

When Alexander Diving Bell invented the xenophone
I heard his voice calling, 'The sea! The sea!'
Hollowly into a shell
As if he could contact Robert Louis Verne
Or all the impossible, massed, forlorn spirits
Edinburgh exiled, waving from twenty thousand leagues

Under force eights the Lusitania,
Hood, Tirpitz, Mary Rose lie barnacled,
Cell-like binnacles of another life
Lost to the world above but frozen here
Among squid, mantas, coral, nameless shoals
Writhing in a lurid, marine Somme

Is the sea Scottish? What are the oceans' flags?
Britannia is ash on the surface of the waves;
We commend   the deep
In   mem
Dot dot dot dash dash dash dot dot dot
            aere peren

Almost meaninglessly vulnerable
To men who hold them with incomprehension
Softened by love, small crania nestle in tweed
Until a woman comes, a maid, a nurse
With her efficient, separating smile
Allowing cigar smoke, whiskies, broadsheet papers

Breastfeeding women soldier
Lovingly, intimately, hurt
Night after night in private dawn campaigns,
Babies in regiments, the Royal Scots Greys,
The Fusiliers, the Guards, madonnas, children,
Waterloo, Sebastopol, Verdun

'Why me?' I cried when Cecco died, 'Why you?'
'Why you?' echoed St Andrews cliffs, 'Why me?'
Sounds of my voice and of my voice re-echoed
You–me, me–you sieved through the bells of flowers,
Merged with sea-urchins, stairwells, conches,
Telephoned through grasses, filtering inside

Hay stalks, through woods and coffee pots
Soundwaves of me and you acoustically
Married plunged beneath St Andrews Bay
Out among lobsters, creels, beneath the hulls
Of homing Fifies sailing by the stars,
Bonded, faithful, never-answered cries

Fed through bakelite receivers, new
Technologies of machines and genes, systems
Replicating, generating, creating
Heavens of sea-slugs, ganglion-by-ganglion maps
Linking you to me, me–you,
Cecco . . . I am dying to hear you

Caravans of beasts cross the sea floor
Battling; there should be more tomes like Forbes's
History of British Starfishes,
More unignorable music like my baby's
'Stennynennynennynennynenny'
Vibraphoned with the long pibrochs of whales

Next, we'll be remixed as a strange city
Where the dead one spring day are allowed
Visits to the living, but gilled under the waves
Where none can breathe, where riverine
Currents of cold meet a persistent Gulf
Stream, thawing a cryogenic, living flood

Sanctioning *in vitro* fertilization, I shoal
Cell by cell by cell by cell by cell
Teeming with breathless nanosecond fins
Deluged with algorithms, difference engines, mouths
Kneading me into new shapes – tendrils, snout–neb,
Gills – and, while this happens,

I write *Katie Stewart* and *The Quiet Heart*,
The Perpetual Curate, menstruate, conduct
Business by telegraph, crisscross Europe, trill
Coloratura Italian names for carp,
Starfish and flounders, chant to squid about
Cosi fan tutte, *Rigoletto*, Siena

Where my husband's buried and where I watched my baby
Die in my arms; I am pulverisingly
Penniless, fortunate, and very tired;
In the early hours, weathered by children's breathing,
Chapters drift up among sluggish cuttlefish,
I see the passing lights of hulls above

Dull skies hanging low, but to the East
Hints of clearness, the light on the Bell Rocks
And at Arbroath, I watched the water-snakes,
They moved in tracks of shining white,
And when they reared, their elfish light
Fell off in hoary flakes

I am my own autobiography
Drafted with children nibbling at the page,
Clamouring, immaturely loud, dividing
Concentration, some quick and some dead,
O Cecco, Tiddy, Maggie, Marjorie,
I extrude your names as wormcasts on Fife's shores

Writing underwater I can be
Protean with shimmer and cascade,
Waxy and oaten, tearful,
Ambered, leylined, Atlantean, coursing
Dolphin-nuzzled, keen and adjectival,
Never to be netted or ticked off

Sea-surges nurse and cradle with me, to-froing
Diaphragms of water laugh, lullabying caves
Gargle the ocean, articulating waves'
Propulsive jokiness coming and going in squirts,
Margaret Oliphant Wilson Oliphant,
I am, babies, I am

I am a pearl and Scotland is a pearl,
Chuckies on the beach, each one a pearl,
Mudie's Circulating Library's
Books turn to pearl, spill out across the floor,
Glasgow's dour drinkers' spit shines for an instant,
Skrechled, tubercular seed-pearl nebulae

Sea water is all starts, an embryonic
Florilegium of lucent drifts,
Pulling, insistent, ceramic-glazed but soft,
Filtering light in snaily, Pictish spirals,
Irises, fannings, anemones, blurred nodes
Unfurling in the tidal give and give

Ossianic, nacre-rich, transforming,
Oceanic, ram-stam, brooking no stop,
Nation-like, yelling and rallying,
Subsiding, calm and violent, perjink
Splashed across headlines, Scotland, Scotland, Scotland
Quartz-strewn, Laurasian, pre-continental

Soften and turn to me, and slowly flower,
Fresh irises, sea pinks, forget-me-nots;
I'll fade away, profound, forgotten, growing
Pearlier beneath the Arran sun
I'll rise to be my land's loveliest necklace
Of Margarets, scattered, spilling far wee stars

Dear Mr Blackwood, here is a short story
Dear Mr Blackwood, here is my *Kirsteen*
Dear Mr Blackwood, my review is finished
Dear Mr Blackwood, I enclose one lung
Dear Mr Blackwood, here is my baby's coffin
Dear Mr Blackwood, say that I am brave

Non-voices emerge from slush of tidal muds,
Pied and shaley, or from singing sands'
'   !'
Coming to me as a medium crying
Childishly, childlessly, for five lost children,
Sperm speckling agate, mealy discolourations,
Random, dark flecks held in tortoiseshell

C.V.: M. O. is born in Wallyford
Now her family moves to Liverpool
Now she suffers a broken engagement's silence
Now, twenty-one, she publishes a novel
Now she visits Edinburgh, woos Blackwood
Now she marries sad Frank who designs stained glass

Now she gives birth (a baby girl) in London,
Maggie, now a puir wee thing who dies,
Now a son dead after one long evening
Now another son, Etonian Tiddy,
Now a fifth child, Stephen (d., influenza)
Now Frank dies, now Cecco is born

Now Maggie dies, now Margaret drowns in novels,
Writing while her last surviving children
Play around her, or wave from a barouche's
Switzerland/Jerusalem/Eton/Balliol College;
Tiddy dies, then Cecco; she writes
'The Library Window', 'A Beleaguered City'

Where the dead brush lithely past the living,
Fussily depart, return, like trains
Depart, return, depart, 25 June
1897, Mrs Oliphant
Passes; I see her mobbed by lugworms,
Bass and elvers, 100% gleg

Dear Mr Murray,
                    Our language should be gendered,
Making the following proudly masculine:
Vending machines, trees, typewriter ribbons,
Cups, semolina, while we would still speak
Of ships as 'she', along with mathematics;
Some surprises too, as Italians say

Il soprano (masculine) or in France
Penis is fem.; then, my dear Mr Murray,
Talk would flow much more pleasurably through
Amniotic diction, a real heart-throb
Philology that swilled and swirled and sworled,
Aye your faithful savante,
                    Lover of Words

Since 'Margaret' = 'pearl', I love to dream
To Bizet's music of a great pearl fished
From Tay, or Spey, or tropical in flarelight
White with clams found by divers in the Gulf
Off Qatar deep in elephantine darkness
Surfacing with tiny globes of light

Some people hate my style's stop-start
North Sea sun-chill, a shoal veering away,
Sighted, lost, slyly looping back
In medias res; my life like yours is
Conch-shaped, a diagram of the human ear
Straining to catch my own repeated name

Sing me map references – long, measured numbers
Pinpointing sandbars on lined nautical charts
Telescopes and periscopes have checked;
Let me read materialist spirits,
The Theology of Oceanography,
Innumerable Worlds, *The Birth of Life*

Fallen in love with the capricious dirt
Of Scotland where a man's a man now I
Hymn angelfishes' aquadynamic hush,
Salmons' effort; my epithalamia slocken;
Sea erodes natural amphitheatres,
Sootily Glasgow slips beneath the waves

Trapped air bursts out of Sauchiehall Street rooms,
Bubbling wildly upwards, tenemental grime
Flakes off and masses on the inky surface;
All the streetlamps fizzle and go out
But on the seabed shops unlock their shutters,
Couples uncertainly begin to dance

Round the submarine telegraph; share prices,
Dates, loves, scientific formulae
Mingle and shine among briny, gum-eyed beasts;
Sea cucumbers, Reuters, brittle-stars,
Editions of my novels, comb-jelly, *The Times*
Recirculate through washed, clean, air-free rooms

Nothing is solid, schist, sandstone, and chert,
Ovoids of granite, rock anemones,
Light-beams' white spots on red serpentine –
All have been molten, flowed as softly
As the Kinness Burn, amber and carnelian,
Chalcedony, bud-petals of the earth

Open around me, a hard-won bouquet
Held in triumph in my own marquee
Ordered to celebrate full fifty years
Writing for *Blackwoods*; pert champagne corks pop
Slàinte! Cheers! Salut! MRS OLIPHANT REQUESTS
THE PLEASURE OF THE CREATURES OF THE SEA

Scotland has never seen democracy;
History: Red Comyn's wife's demeaning wail
Over her children, through rich, spirituous rain
Soaking a slaughter on imperial fields,
Pissed regiments; I want some dignity
For the unmaimed in a democratic land

Buy Mrs Oliphant's *The Chronicles of Carlingford!*
'An assured success' 'A work of great delight'
'Splendidly touching' 'A domestic jewel'
'Her translation of Montalembert will live forever'
Vellum 3 vols. Octavo First Edition
Come buy! Come buy! Come buy!

Father Almighty, I strive against thee;
I reproach thee; I do not submit;
Maggie, if you would but rap the table
Once, if I could but hear your quiver
In the medium's voice; routine starts up again;
Impossibly, Our Father, I endure

Pay me; I work; I will not be your necklace
Till you adorn me with creeled villages,
Arisaig, Morar, Crail, and Anstruther
Polished and strong, until I cast them off
One by one, slowly, in apocalypse,
Turning to wink then walk into the sea

Wee lovely, terrifying, imperious people,
Why did you die still in your knitted shawls,
Nursed, longed-for, fed? I'm crying
Over nothing, over an emptiness
Only I notice, my big, ridiculous name
Owling back to haunt your minute graves

I see a red-haired girl on the losing side
Always marching in a tartan toorie,
Skirt, strong shoes, down vennels of Scots towns,
Campaigning for democracy, my country
Right and wrong, she wears a cardboard breastplate
Proudly, with painted block caps, VOTES FOR WOMEN

Scotland, your Mary is a Margaret,
Shod in ultramarine, bangled with whelks;
Knox is my muse, his monstrous regimen
Landlubbed, declaiming on the Firth of Forth;
Non-swimmers' emblem, he wobbles, presbyterian,
Tiptoeing on chuckies; I pout him kisses of spume

Now the great winds shoreward blow,
Now the salt tides seaward flow;
Now the wild white horses play,
Champ and chafe and toss in the spray . . .
Children dear, was it yesterday
(Call yet once) that he went away?

Birth overbalances men, pitching them forward
A generation; balance-sheets slip from their hands
Pleasurably; a father birling round
Laughs to be ungainly, heavy-suited,
Dancing in the privacy of being with babies,
Emancipated, masculated, light

Roles for daddies: hedge-bearded, adamantine,
Fiercely crabbit, crouched behind their 'No!'
Or louche and yissless, slipping like a drink
Poured back down the bottle's green neck, spilt away,
Lost; I am a father and a mother
Underneath the waves of Pegwell Bay

Marriage: dappled light through red stained-glass
Gloving a limb, jewelling us, rich
Spectra coating and nacring everyday
Troubles: his tubercular, fathering voice,
'Now sleeps the crimson petal, now the white;
Nor waves the cypress in the palace walk;

Nor winks the gold fin in the porphyry font:
The fire-fly wakens: waken thou with me';
I woke in peeling, impasto Siena,
Frank gone; in hot, holy Jerusalem,
Frank gone; I am a single, married woman
Impatient with the surface of the earth

As the sea circles this planet's
Pictish spirals, Celtic solar discs,
World-snake popping its tail in its own mouth,
So I perfect my impossible, nuanced grit,
Nacring its pregnant shell, its given/giving
360°

LIGLAG

It's sniauvin i the Howe o Alford;
Whaiskin liggars are wede awa.

A' wark's twa-handit-wark this season,
Screens daurk as a hoodie craw.

Torry-eaten databases
Yield scotch mist o an auld leid,

Bodwords, bodes, thin scraelike faces.
Peter an Major Cook are deid.

Nemms o places haud thir secrets,
Leochel-Cushnie, Lochnagar,

Luvely even untranslatit,
Cast-byes unnerneath the haar

Dreepin doon tae Inverbervie
When the haert's as grit's a peat.

Youtlin souns blaw frae the glebe.
Pour a dram an tak it neat,

Neat as Cattens, Tibberchindy,
Tomintoul or Aiberdeen,

Mapped an scanned, a karaoke
O gangrel souns I ken hae been

Mapread an spoken by my faither
I mony a cowpissed bield, a Bank

O Scotlan, or a Baltic dawn.
Skourdaboggie, auld an lank,

I key them intae this computer's
Empire by a taskit wa.

Peterculter, Maryculter.
Tine haert, tine a'. Tine haert, tine a'.

SENSATION OF ANOTHER LANGUAGE

*It's snowing in the Howe of Alford; gasping violently for breath,
salmon that have lain too long in the fresh water are weeded out.
All work is second-rate work that needs redoing in this season,
screens dark as a carrion crow. Databases that are like exhausted
land give up the small but wetting rain of an old language,
traditional sayings expressing the fate of a family, portents, thin
faces like shrivelled shoes. Peter and Major Cook are dead.
Names of places hold their secrets, Leochel-Cushnie, Lochnagar,
lovely even untranslated, stuff thrown away as unserviceable
underneath the sea-mist dripping down to Inverbervie when the
heart is ready to burst with sorrow. Feeble sounds, like those of
dying animals, come from the field by the manse. Pour a dram
and take it neat, neat as Cattens, Tibberchindy, Tomintoul or
Aberdeen, mapped and scanned, a karaoke of wandering sounds
I know have been mapread and spoken by my father in many a
shelter pissed on by cows, a Bank of Scotland, or a Baltic dawn.
Like the last surviving member of a family, old and spare, I key
them into this computer's empire beside a wall fatigued with hard
work. Peterculter, Maryculter. If you let sorrow overcome you, you
lose everything. If you let sorrow overcome you, you lose
everything.*

DEINCARNATION

Each daybreak laptops siphon off the glens,
Ada, Countess of Lovelace, Vannevar Bush,

Alan Turing spectral in Scourie,
Babbage downloading half of Sutherland

With factors and reels, inescapable
Whirring of difference engines.

Inverailort and Morar host
Shrewd pioneers of computing.

Digitized, blue, massive Roshven
Loses its substance, granite and grass

Deincarnated and weightless.
Shaking hands with absentees,

Beaters, gutters have their pockets emptied
Of any last objects, even a nanomachine,

A pebble, a lucky coin.
Skulking on Celtic Twilight shores,

Each loch beyond is cleared of itself,
Gaelic names, flora, rainfall

So close, the tangible spirited away,
Cybered in a world of light.

ALFORD

Blearily rummaging the internet,
Aged thirty eight, not knowing where I was,
I found a site designed as an old harled manse,

Sash windows opening on many Scotlands.
Through one surf broke on the West Sands, St Andrews,
And through another Glasgow mobbed George Square.

Templeton carpets fluttered up and clucked:
Crevecoeurs, La Fleches, azeels, minorcas,
Cochins, Langshans, Scots dumpies, Cornish game.

The hallstand's canny, digitized gamp
Pointed to fading pixels; when I touched them
I felt *The Poultry-Keeper's Vade-Mecum*,

Though in the next room, where a bren-gun spat,
Its title changed into *King's Regulations*;
Tanks manoeuvred round the hearth and range,

Smashing duck eggs, throwing up clouds of flour.
Fleeing the earth-floored kitchen, an ironing table
Hirpled like girderwork from bombed Cologne

Into the study where my Aunt Jean studied
How not to be a skivvy all her life,
While my dead uncle revved his BSA,

Wiping used, oily hands on Flanders lace.
Ministers primed themselves in Jesus's Greek.
Bankers shot pheasants. Girls sang. My father

Walked me through presses with a map of Paris,
Though all the names he used were Cattens, Leochil,
Tibberchindy, Alford, Don, Midmill.

I understood. 'Virtual reality?'
I asked him. In reply he looked so blank
His loved face was a fresh roll of papyrus

Waiting to be made a sacred text,
Hands empty as the screen where he projected
Slides of our holidays at Arisaig,

His body fresh cotton sheets in the best bedroom
Of his boyhood home before he was a boy.
Waiting here, he waits to meet my mother,

For a first date at St Martin in the Fields.
Here, his father, Robert, catches light
On his own deathbed, pipe and *Press and Journal*

Combusting in a way none can control.
Manse rooms huddle, fill with shetland ponies,
London tubes. There is no here. Here goes.

En te oikia tou Patros mou monai pollai eisin:
In my Father's house are many mansions:
If it were not so, I would have told you.

FIAT LUX

Let there be braziers, holophotal lenses,
Polished golden flags, champagne and candles,

Let rays shine through the rose window of Chartres,
Let there be cowslips, myriad splats of rain,

Trilobites, new parliaments, red neon,
Let there be twin-stone rings and mirrorglass

Skyscrapers, glinting jumbos, Rannoch lochans
In which huge skies can touch down in the sun.

Let there be Muckle Flugga's phallic pharos,
Bug-eyed, winking tree-frogs; let there be

Grand Canyons, fireflies, tapers, tapirs, matches
Good and bad, simply to fan the flames.

Let there be lasers, Fabergé crystal eggs,
Hens' squelchy yolks, birch-bark's thin,

Diaphanous scratchiness, let there be you,
Me, son and daughter, let the Rhine

Flow through Cologne and Basle, let there be
Victoria Falls, Great Zimbabwe, hornets' wings,

Angels, cardboard, zinc, the electric brae.
Let there be both stromatolites and cows,

Llamas and zebras, dromedaries, cats,
Bens, buns and banns, let there be all,

End all, every generation, so the whole
Unknown universe be recreated

Through retinal cone and iris and religion.
As has been said before, let there be light.

CREDO

As a candle-flame believes in the speed of light
I believe in you.

As the shoelace of glass believes in the full grown eel
I believe in you.

As Perth in Australia believes in Perth in Scotland,
As an old hand's vein believes in a baby's wrist,

Since what we cannot speak about we must,
As worlds have done, still do, will do, I make

For you, to you, in you, now and through this
My declaration of dependence.

THE TIP OF MY TONGUE

Some days I find, then throw my voice
Deep down the larynx of Glen Esk,

Ears cocked to catch what rumbles back,
English-Scots-Gaelic hailstones.

Other days the tip of my tongue
Is further off than Ayers Rock.

I'm lost for words, or find inside them
A pentecost that isn't tuned in.

I dream I'm a Shetland winterlight
Shining where you drowse in your nightdress,

Dreaming too, your book beside you,
 In your hair an aigrette of ferns and beads of rain.

Enough said. Or of waking at a lover's angle
With you on the tip of my tongue.

CONJUGATION

I love the bigamy of it, the fling
Of marriage on top of marriage.
Marry me, Alice, marry my secrets,
Sight unseen, and marry Glasgow and Rose
Macaulay and the snell east wind.
I'll marry you and Iona and has-been,
Shall-be firths of slipways and dwammy kyles.
I do, you did, we'll do, hitched to every last
Drop of our wedding-day showers,
Downpours, reflecting us over and over,
So we'll fall in compact mirrors, blebs
As the heavens open, bride's veil, grey suit, ringing
Wet with carillons of rain.
That day seems like only tomorrow,
Present, future, pluperfect, perfect smirr
Champagning us doon the watter, on,
Launching us, conjugating each haugh,
Oxter, pinkie and lobeless lug
As it will be in the beginning.

ARBUTHNOTT

Gales churn cornfields to a golden stushie,
North Sea haar dooks the North Sea.

Later, from Kinneff round past Dunnottar,
Heat vectors everywhere. Sunned kirks surmount

Peninsulas of cloud, wisps of the land.
Sound is a Triumph Herald, crickets. South,

Brechin Round Tower soars, a slim
Minaret of the Mearns.

On the swings, one minute
Feet on the ground, the next all up in the air,

I catch how Kincardineshire sky's
Transvaalish, Budapesty, Santa Barbaran,

Zurich on a perfect day. I love the North East
Everywhere of it, how it just zeros

On and on, then flauchters back
So zircon, so azure, so Alice blue.

PILGRIM

for Alice

Lighter than a snailshell from a thrush's anvil,
Glimpsed in grass cuttings, whiffs of splintered light,

But knee-tough, toddler-fierce and undeflected,
Slogging between Arbirlot and Balmirmer

Where the Arbroath road shoogles in the heat,
All plainchant and sticky willie,

E-babble and cushie doos,
A soul, like the signal from a mobile phone,

Heads south where muscadine light
Slurs mile-long midsummer breakers,

And sings out, blithe, by a kirk whose bellrope
Hangs, a frayed leash that's attached to the whole of the sky.

ST ANDREWS

I love how it comes right out of the blue
North Sea edge, sunstruck with oystercatchers.
A bullseye centred at the outer reaches,
A haar of kirks, one inch in front of beyond.

A MOMENT OF YOUR TIME

for Kate Whiteford

Z-rods and a Pictish hoopla of carved rings
Swim into view. Yachtsails on the North Sea
Tack back and forth, xeroxing other summers
When other yachtsails did that too, sped, idled,
Veered into light. Dwamtime. Heat-haze. Relaxed,
Unchronological ribbed fields. Leylines
Flounce across territories never ours,
Where we belong. Grassed-over souterrains
Rich with mud-rhythms, moss-haired residues
Of moon and beaver, lily, loon and quine,
I praise you all. Wind-sough, wind-sook
Of chamber-music, cairn-singing, firths'
Haar threaded through a net, babbling with dew,
Murmur me, let me catch another's breath,
Lightly, as part of breathing. Here it is:
Remnant, keepsake, rune, God-given script
Made just for you, the right lines, sacred text
Of matter cooked in stars, instantly endless,
Then passing on but holding nothing back,
Good for the child, the skeletal, the green
Foliage-bank whose sap's stared into at
Eye level. Here's the whole shebang that is
Time, place and climate, ebbing, dancing, set
In stone and motion, calmly at the ready
Before and after, purled in helices,
Every last atom pregnant with an A.

THE BAD SHEPHERD

I am the bad shepherd, torching my flocks in the fields,
Feeding them accelerant, hecatombs of wedders and tups.
In pits or pyres all are sheared and shamed by the flames.
Every sheep is a black sheep in that fire,
Penned in by heat, conspicuously consumed.
If one escapes when ninety-nine are burned,
Hunt it down. Best now my lambs are lost
So sheep are shelved, or vaporised unsold,
Hanging in charred clouds – hairst hogs, maillies, and crocks.
Cloned palls cover Cumbria. Shadows slur Lockerbie's drumlins.
Cling, braxy, scrapie, tremmlin, pindling, all
Diseases of sheep go huddled together in one
Beltane burn. *Ca' the yowes to the knowes* . . .
I am the bad shepherd. Follow me.

THE AULD ENEMY

There they are, bonny fechters, rank on tattery rank,
Murderer-saints, missionaries, call-centre workers, Tattoos,
Bunneted tartans weaving together
Darkest hours, blazes of glory,
Led by a First Bawheid, rampant, hair fizzin, sheepsheared,
Scrummin doon, pally wi their out-of-town allies,
Wallace fae Califaustralia, Big Mac, an Apple Mac,
Back from the backwoods, wi Rob Fergusson, Hume, Sawney Bean –
See how yon lot yawn and yell and stretch
Right owre from Blantyre tae Blantyre, Malawi!
Wait till ye catch the whites o their eyes, aye,
The specky, pinky-flecky whites o their eyes
Worn out from ogling down a Royal Mile o microscopes, or fou
Wi dollars n yen signs, or glaikit wi bardic blindness. Wait
Till ye hear their 'Wha daur meddle wi me', their hoochs
And skirls of 'Rigour!' Wait till ye smell
Through coorse, dauntless, distilled Jock courage,
The wee, trickling smell of their underdog-on-the-make fear
Dribbling down greaves, rusting nicked, spancelled armour.
Wait till you hear the start of those whispers,
'We're fine, thanks, Tony.' 'Don't rock the boat.'
'Oh, thank you, thank you, Secretary of State.'
That's the time, eyeball-to-eyeball,
Tae face them down, the undefeated
Canny Auld Enemy, us.

PLANETIST

I love all windy, grand designs, all blashes
Splattering the dark, heaving the moon

High over spruces, under the weathered
Cloud rivers turning in their beds.

From the tip of my tongue to the pit of my stomach,
From my eyeballs to the balls of my heels

With my lanky body I thee worship,
Scotland, New Zealand, all national dots,

The salt of the earth, the pepper of the earth,
The oregano of the world –

But I'm a planetist as well,
Singing your praises, honoured speck,

Stung with sleepless inspiration
When even the wind has emphysema,

Roads, keep right on to the end of yourselves,
Islands, keep your heads above water.

MONS MEG

for my daughter

Under warmed, antiseasonal skies
Zoo capercailzies flap away

Towards the terminus of species;
Headsetted tourists evolve into

Cyborgs on the Castle ramparts;
But I have ears and eyes only for you,

Wee ballerina, pas-de-bas-ing in front of Mons Meg,
Singing down the barrel of that gun.

I love how you yell a pirouette,
'Hullo, Mons Meg! Goodbye, Mons Meg!'

Blithe beside its heavy, pitch-black muzzle,
Laughing in the cannon's mouth.

BIRTHPLACE

translated from the Latin of Arthur Johnston (1587–1641)

Here, neck and neck with the Vale of Tempe,
Stretches the Howe of the Johnstons.
Underneath Aberdeenshire sky
The sparkling, silvery Urie Burn
Slaloms over well-fed farms.
Benachie's sgurr untousles a last quiff of cloud;
Night and day hang in the balance.
The Don hides garnets. The high glens, too,
Dazzle with gemstones, pure as India's best.
Nature reclines *au naturel*
On a surging bed of heather. Swallows
Loop in the tangy air. Salmon
Flicker. Strong-bodied cattle
Chew the cud in the pastures.
Here, where northern apples redden,
Cornfields bend under golden grain,
Largesse lets orchards sag.
I sprang from this, these rivers, fields
Over a hundred generations
Always the Howe of the Johnstons.
Virgil made his birthplace famous;
Mine will be the making of my poems.

GLASGOW

translated from the Latin of Arthur Johnston (1587–1641)

Head held high among sister cities,
Glasgow, you are a star.
Gulf Stream winds defrost you. No fear, though,
Of your being frazzled to a crisp at high noon.
The Clyde sweeps through, detoxed like amber,
A thousand ships flying your flag.
Ashlar bridges you, bank to wet bank,
Granting all comers safe passage.
Round about, orchards and roses
Up the Clyde Valley, a Paestum of the distant west,
Woodnymphs, each lithe as a salmon.
Town centre tenements' flashbulb brilliance
Hides wall-to-wall Style; sheer marble
Churches to die for. Down the road
Rat-a-tat patter stuns the Sheriff Court.
Bang in the middle, your University
Sings hymns to Phoebus Apollo.
You make the gods grin, my favourite Glasgow.
Sea, earth and air have ganged up to make you shine.

ST ANDREWS

translated from the Latin of Arthur Johnston (1587–1641)

Sacred St Andrews, the whole wide world
Saw you as the burgh of God.
Jove, eyeing your great Cathedral,
Blushed for his own wee Tarpeian kirk.
The architect of the Ephesian temple,
Seeing yours, felt like a fake.
Culdee priests in holy cassocks
Gazed through your East Neuk of light.
St Andrews' Archbishop, clad in gold,
Bellowed at Scotland's Parliament.
Now that's gone, walls ankle-high,
Priestly *fiat lux* tarnished.
Still you pull poets, though. You wow
Lecturers and lab technicians.
Aurora of the Peep o' Day in Fife
Frisks ashore with salt-reddened fingers,
Herring-sparkle of dawn.
Thetis coughs through 10 a.m. haar,
Waking hirpling, hungover students
Who sober up with golfclubs.
Phocis was Phoebus's long-time lover,
Attica of Pallas. In St Andrews
Each dances. Forever. Now.

TO ROBERT BARON

translated from the Latin of Arthur Johnston (1587–1641)

Dear Doctor Baron, Aberdeen,
Read this, my mudstained, gloomy work
Sent from a burn that feeds the Don.
Out on my croft, far out of town,
Among rough, stony, worn-out fields,
Ex-poet, and ex-learned man,
I plough my furrow with dour beasts.
Bent double, eyes glued to the clods,
I trek behind my oxen's lines,
Goading them on or chanting verse,
Teaching the ox boustrophedon.

Sometimes I hoe and hoe the marl,
Sometimes I harrow it to death,
Or jab it. With my writing hand
I haul the stones from new-ploughed fields
Then, maybe, irrigate the land,
Or drain it with a shallow pit.
Both arms ache with threshing crops,
Both feet are just about done in.
Stripped off, I fork muck with a graip,
Then spread dung on the heavy soil.
Arcturus winks. I scythe my crops.

Some of the harvest's scorched, ground down,
Some of it's in the Gadie burn.
Through the hot summer I prepare
For snow, cutting and banking peat.
Excavating the earth's bowels
I just about see spooks and think
The dead peer back. What makes it worse,
As when a storm first hits and then
Wave after wave pounds in, my head's
Just touched the pillow in pitch dark
When I'm awoken by the lark.

My overalls are shaggy pelts.
Breakfast's a turnip once again,
The Gadie burn to wash it down.
I'm dying in a thousand ways –
The Underworld might cheer me up –
So lonely, scared the mirror shows
Not who I was. Teeth like a dog's,
Hair dandruff-white, boils on my lips,
I take my stand knee-deep in shite,
Bowed-down, too harnessed to the plough,
Downcast, the beast I have become.

CEUD MILE FAILTE

Iain Crichton Smith, 1928–1998

This morning I stare at frosty wavelets,
Expecting you to bob up,

Your silkie's head, hazel-bald and polished
In a spry wig of dulse, adrift between

Beijing and Garrabost, Yarmouth and South Australia,
Canada and Taynuilt, Paris and the village of Bayble,

Buoyed beside heroic tatters
Of Lewis or Harris, their gneiss and quartz

End-on to force elevens, sparkling.
Drowned learner choirs, sea-booted, garbling school
    hymns,

Haunt that white house through whose doorway you
    float,
Chatting with your friends in one room in English,

Calling to the others in Gaelic.
Your language lives with a tube down its gullet.

For every hundred thousand welcomes
An abrupt hundred thousand goodbyes.

FROM THE TOP

for Iain Galbraith

From the top, breathless, feet in the clouds,
I see how at the ankle-high horizon

Dutch fields are Berber rugs in a bazaar;
Red tiled roofs pave the village far below;

I clock the non-stop Colorado River,
Dandelion heads unblown in East Westphalia,

Bings, sunlit mesas of the Scottish Lowlands,
Stretching towards nettled woods whose watermills'

Dust harps, thick burr stones, and dark gavelocks
Promise half firlots or a grinding halt.

I spot South Island beckoning Amazonia
Past Arrochar and Wiesbaden, I watch

Shackleton's shadow cross the Southern Lights
And swallows brushing Arabic on air,

That canny man of 78 who built
The biggest sugar mills in Puerto Rico,

Horn spoons, a rotting, gnawed-at Hong Kong torso,
And Carrick Castle inlaid on Loch Goil,

All things improbable, as God's my witness,
Bamiyan Buddhas, Easter Island heads,

And everything I see here from the top
Is overlooked by bens and glens of stars.

WINDFARMING

Flailing outstretched cirrus fields,
Sleek metals throw up their hands,

Gleaning, milling where there is no corn
In the agribusiness of air,

Totempoled into acceleration's
Ultimate source and resource,

Propeller-driven crosses of the risen Christ,
Great ghosts of standing stones.

While everything is speeding up,
Overheating, hurtling away,

Good to stand still on this moonlit upland,
Canny, uncanny, with a choir of angels

Towering above us, beating their wings,
Piloting the earth on its way.

TREE DANCE

Dandering through Glen Convinth woods,
Fro and to, there and here,
I give up trying not to slip. A frog
Plops into hiding. Just about lost, I inch
Close to a pine and stare up its bark's
Arterial road to the clouds.
I lean against the dry, encrusted trunk,
My ear an inch from rings and resin, hiding,
Frog-quiet, out of the wind. All give,
There and here, to and fro
The tree sways, dandering in high blashes, rooted.
I sway with it, cheek to living cheek.
Each of us will last a lifetime.

THE ORDER

After a partnership that failed
Near dreich Port Glasgow, now at Yoker all

Went like a dream: the order
A sleek-hulled steam yacht for a German client

Due to be launched in late 1914.
That was the spring my mother's uncle sweated

And did not stop. He and his staggering wife
Went by unsteady train to Greenock West

To be looked after by my grandmother
Berthed in a tenement. Enteric fever.

He died, but the women lived through the Great War,
Which, though she was not thought of at Versailles,

Stopped just three years before my mother's birth;
And by the time her fluent Pitman's shorthand

Reached ninety words a minute, a bomb fell,
Blitzing the Greenock flat she had just left.

Next it's my turn, part of the post-War years,
Leverets scooting, fast as twanged elastic,

The shipyards closed, and, like an open book,
My young son can explain the human genome,

Letting me see in unassembled brass
Screws, handrails, greased pistons of an engine,

Bow-wave and wake, the stranded DNA
Of boatbuilding, that unbuilt yacht, the order.

UIST

South in the north, sun clasped inside the rain,
Levitational birdsong in low fields;

While e-mails graze sand-covered villages
And shaped bone combs comb force-fives in the dunes

I lie down parallel with Grenitote,
Wellies to Udal, head in kidney vetch,

Watching the sly clouds' micromanagement
Of thirty shades of cerulean blue.

June gales have singed the yellow irises,
And frittered silage bags. Behind a croft

Native, cross-bred Hebridean sheep
Scratch themselves on a satellite dish.

Rain's on its way, and so are tides on theirs;
I catch them up, and start to stride across

The machair, thinking of Taigh Chearsabhagh
Where in the sleek museum New Age lettering

Englishes a maybe age-old Gaelic gnomon:
There is no stone but the stream will change its shape.

BLUE SONG

(made by Mary, daughter of Red Alasdair,
soon after she was left in Scarba)
after the Gaelic of Mary MacLeod (c.1615–1705)

Hoireann o

I am sad
since a week ago

left on this island,
no grass, no shelter.

If I could
I'd get back home,

making the journey
rightaway

to Ullinish
of white-hoofed cattle

where I grew up,
a little girl

breast-fed there
by soft-palmed women,

in the house of brown-haired Flora,
Lachlan's daughter,

milkmaid
among the cows

of Roderick Mor
MacLeod of the banners.

I have been happy
in his great house,

living it up
on the dancefloor,

fiddle-music
making me sleepy,

pibroch
my dawn chorus.

Hoireann o ho bhi o,
Ro hoireann o o hao o.

Say hullo for me
to Dunvegan.

CROY. EE. GAW. LONKER. PIT.

Croy. Ee. Gaw. Lonker. Pit.
Croy: an animal pen, a rained-on pigsty
Snorting with mooning bums of bacon, snouts
Spikehaired, buxom, Pictish-beasty, rank.
Croy. Ee. Gaw. Lonker. Pit.
Croy: Once, dogging off a dig on the Antonine Wall,
Knees-to-chin in the back of a Beetle near Croy,
I eyed a triumphal arch of Castlecary's
British Empire viaduct above
Turfed-over Roman barracks. Soil had sunk
Castellum, *praetorium*, and *via*.
Then, *en route* to a *plein air* Latin milestone,
Illegally crossing the motorway,
The car stalled. That coachbuilder with Alexander's Buses,
Spare-time diviner, dowser for lost wells and oak roots,
Revved the engine, stalled the Beetle again
Side-on in front of two great racing lorries.
All five of us, inside our billiard ball,
Unlearned language, trapped in a single breath's
Kyrie eleison, Kyrie eleison
Watching those wall-cabbed artics bearing down
Horns blaring, *AAAAAAAAAAAAAA*,
Doing eighty. Then our engine started.
Ee: an eye, a loophole, a way out,
An opening for water, a delight;
Ee: the eye-opening silent noise of e-mail,
That interruption from another world.
Croy. Ee. Gaw. Lonker. Pit.
Gaw: a Fife word for a drainage furrow.
I walk each day past rows of Pictish graves.
Fife Council's laying mud-brown plastic drainpipes
Down the dead-straight leyline of a Pictish road.
Croy. Ee. Gaw. Lonker. Pit.

Lonker: a hole in a wall, a *yett* through which
Sheep may slip, or a burn, a stream flow under.
Every wall, from Hadrian's to dry-stane-dyke,
Longs for a lonker's
Huddled, nervous rush of living fleece
Against its whinstane, a *vindauga*, a wind's eye, a window
To see through, snow's gurgling, flushing *slàinte!*
Of ice-melt, babbling its lost language,
Baby-talking its way through the WHO GOES THERE?
Croy. Ee. Gaw. Lonker. Pit.
SPEAK ENGLISH! PLAIN ENGLISH! *Naw* . . .
Cry the orphaned *hwll* of *Croy. Ee. Gaw.*
Thrawnly as a couple long and long for a child,
Hopelessly, edgily, until their own stone opens.
Croy. Ee. Gaw. Lonker. Pit.
Pit: to dig holes, marking an edge.
Pit: a portion, or a piece of land, a homestead,
Pittenweem, Pitmillie, Pittodrie, Pittencrieff.
Pit: the only syllable we know
Was born from the obliterated Pictish language –
One landmark cross, perjink on a drowned spire's tip
Whose minster's carved beasts, whorls, and crucifixes
Lie silted, sunk in a Fife-sized, flooded pit.
Croy. Ee. Gaw. Lonker. Pit.
Croy.
Ee.
Gaw.
Lonker.
Pit.

THE MITHRAEUM

God-mulch. Apollo. Coventina.
Snapped-off moons and pre-Christian crosses

Pit the tor. Come-back king,
Midas-touch Mithras, his moorland shrines

Dank caves or knee-high proto-kirks
Northwest of Hexham, waits

First for microbial, then feather-thin,
Then skull-thick, unscabbarded dawn

Butchering the bull-black darkness,
Cutting Christmas Eve's throat.

Mithraic puddles freeze to a golden crunch.
Roads' black ice catches the light.

Hollowed out of the altar's back,
Space for a ceremonial lamp

Set to shine through the holes that petal
Mithras's sun-round head,

From sheep-pee daybreak to sodden gloaming
Keeping the faiths'

Fire lit through ear-burning, toe-nipping cold,
I am the Light of the World.